Waterlog

Journeys Around An Exhibition

Film and Video Umbrella

Waterlog

'Across what distances in time do the elective affinities and correspondences connect?'

W.G. Sebald *The Rings of Saturn* (1998)

Waterlog: Journeys Around An Exhibition
ISBN: 978-1-904270-24-9
Published by Film and Video Umbrella

© 2007 Film and Video Umbrella,
the artists and the authors

Publication supported by Arts Council England

Journeys Around An Exhi

bition *Foreword*

Steven Bode

'Waterlog' is an exhibition of contemporary artists' work that was staged at Norwich Castle Museum and Art Gallery (and the nearby Sainsbury Centre for Visual Arts) in the first few months of 2007, before travelling to The Collection in Lincoln in the autumn of the same year. Plotting a somewhat circuitous course between two ancient cathedral cities at either edge of the East Anglian fenlands, the project set out to explore the wider landscape of the east of England, with the idea of the literary journey as one of its overarching themes. A guiding presence throughout was the figure of W.G. Sebald, the German-born author who made Norfolk his home before his untimely death in 2001, and whose novel *The Rings of Saturn* (1998) describes an equally meandering circular walk, beginning and ending in Norwich. Sebald's elliptical style—digressive, poetic, reflective—sets the tone of the project as a whole, in which artists' forays out into the surrounding landscape uncover unexpected affinities and connections embedded in the history and geography of the region.

Featuring pieces by Marcus Coates, Tacita Dean, Alec Finlay and Guy Moreton, Alexander and Susan Maris, and Simon Pope, 'Waterlog' consisted entirely of a series of new commissions, each forging a fresh and distinctive path through a richly evocative terrain that is unusually flooded with both water and memory, and the accumulated flotsam of history, and whose ghosts, to which Sebald was particularly attuned, are everywhere you look. In some of the artists' works, there are echoes of the people and places that Sebald encounters in *The Rings of Saturn*. Tacita Dean's film portrait of Michael Hamburger, for example, records a visit to the poet's Suffolk home (in what proved to be the last months of his life) that is uncannily reminiscent of Sebald's own stopover a decade or so earlier. In their lyrical study of the disappearing coastline near Dunwich, Guy Moreton and Alec Finlay tread equally closely in Sebald's footsteps; adding to a long line of writers and artists who have travelled to this haunted shore to sample its melancholy atmosphere and make their own small mark against the encroaching tide. However vivid they appear, these signs of influence or allusion are points of intersection rather than specific acts of illustration; paths that happen to cross, rather than routes that are reverentially followed. Like the boom of the bittern (a bird long associated with East Anglia), whose sonorous call bursts full-throatedly from Marcus Coates' sound work, and whose disputed origin forms one of the many dolorous grace-notes in *The Rings of Saturn*, voices tend to linger in this mysterious landscape, but are often hard to pinpoint explicitly.

What the 'Waterlog' artists share with Sebald is a unifying sensibility: elegiac, enquiring; understated, almost hesitant, for all its seriousness of purpose. It is an outlook, and a set of preoccupations, that is not unique to Sebald, but which reverberates across the work of a number of other writers, some of whom have been drawn, like him, to this corner of the world, or to similar out-of-the-way places, whose easy erudition possesses a comparable grasp of cultural marginalia and minutiae, or whose feel for language has an equally extraordinary knack of not just describing but imprinting a landscape. A particular aim of 'Waterlog' has been to invoke, or involve, a range of other authors, and incorporate them into the wider project, in the way that Sebald's own literary journeys radiate out from their solitary pursuits to assemble their own cast of kindred spirits. Writers who have been formative to its development, or who seemed particularly able to broaden its horizons, appear throughout its various manifestations, as contributors to these pages, or as participants in one of its pivotal pieces, Simon Pope's *The Memorial Walks*. This roll-call of writers is eclectic and wide-ranging, and not everyone is a writer of words—the music of Benjamin Britten, for example, continues to infuse this part of the country, and his legacy is gracefully retraced in Alexander and Susan Maris's *Silentium*. Another name to single out is that

of Roger Deakin, whose 'swimmer's journey through Britain' was unknown to me when I first happened upon what I thought was an appropriate name for a title, and which has since gifted other invaluable insights.

Coinciding with the launch of the project in Lincoln, this publication offers both an informal guide to the exhibition and, in another echo of Sebald, an orbit around its wider subject. Once again, there is an emphasis on newly-commissioned writing: a new poem by Matthew Hollis, and essays by Brian Dillon and Robert Macfarlane, that complement reprinted texts by poet George Szirtes and artist/writers Alec Finlay and Tacita Dean. Like all journeys, 'Waterlog' has been profoundly coloured by the landscape through which it has travelled but equally powerfully illuminated by the people who have both graced and opened up its route. Although I charted its original course, and gave it much of its initial direction, the ground that has been covered would not have been so extensive, or so deftly negotiated, without the involvement of my co-curator, Jeremy Millar. It goes without saying that the road would have been infinitely longer and harder without the support of my colleagues at Film and Video Umbrella, and key people at each of the three venues, notably Nick Thornton, Amanda Geitner and Jill Sullivan. Without a substantial commitment from our various funders, we might not have set off at all—my thanks go especially to Arts Council England, and the Henry Moore Foundation. Special thanks, though, are reserved for the artists (and writers) who have led the way and whose energy and commitment have made this such an enjoyable and rewarding experience.

Waterlog

Alec Finlay and Guy Moreton

Waterlog

Marcus Coates
Tacita Dean
Alexander and Susan Maris
Alec Finlay and Guy Moreton
Simon Pope

Waterlog

Airlocked

Brian Dillon

All things are done in some place; but if we consider place to be no more
but the next hollow superficies of air, alas! how thin and fluid a thing is
air, and how thin a film is a superficies, and a superficies of air!'
John Donne, Meditations

In the writings of W.G. Sebald, it is at times impossible to separate
art from atmosphere: to tell person, place or thing from the air that
surrounds them. It is as if his books were rather weather systems than
agglomerations of words, such is their reliance on meteorological
imagery. Sebald's narrators—already a wavering lot, their outlines
hazy at best—are time and again usurped as storytellers by a succession
of mists, clouds, drizzles and miasmas: one feels as though the weather
itself has been given a voice. The many labyrinthine or monumental
buildings in which Sebald's stand-ins take refuge, or find themselves
wandering without hope, fail to provide airtight defence against
atmospheres that seep through stone and glass, enveloping bodies and
objects in airs that feel weirdly fleshy: plethoric, adipose, mortified.

Thus, for example, the properties of that curious chamber,
the Ladies' Waiting Room at Liverpool Street station, where the
melancholic exile Austerlitz seems to see an 'icy grey light' extinguished
almost as soon as it has sunk into the dusty, subterranean-seeming space.
But it is in *The Rings of Saturn*—the title already adverts to the book's
gaseous concerns—that Sebald truly gives himself over to uncanny
atmospherics. The book wakes, in the dog days, to a 'colourless patch of
sky'; before long the narrator, on a train between Norwich and Lowestoft,
is regarding his fellow passengers through a preternatural half-light. He
later recounts a dream told him by Anne, the wife of his friend Michael
Hamburger, in which, she says, the atmosphere was 'denser than air and
somewhat resembled streaming currents of deep, silent water'.

Air, in Sebald's novels, is a kind of allegorical adhesive:
the elastic medium by which—whether it is the gelid air that he recalls
preceding the hurricane of 1987, or a series of strange ventilation
holes found in a tomb at Ditchingham cemetery—he binds together
the disparate strands of his text. Atmosphere, however, has another
valence in his writings: understood in the sense of a mood, impression
or effect, we might say that Sebald's books are above all *atmospheric*.
His aesthetic of drift and decay, his lugubrious comedy and suffocating
sense of sorrow and loss, the unsettling unity of his digressions—these

all demand an adjective sufficiently precise and capacious as to enclose
the evanescent substance of his narratives. Even the most attentive
and admiring of readers are known to come away from Sebald having
forgotten vast weather fronts of anecdote and discrete flurries of
description, recalling only this stupefying effect, as of some type of
literary ether. Re-reading Sebald is for this reason a constant surprise:
forgotten narrative junctions and overgrown digressions appear out
of the fog with arresting frequency.

  It is partly a matter of style—Sebald's sentences seem
at once extremely considered and concrete, and scarcely there at all.
In *The Rings of Saturn*, describing the vagrant and stately prose of the
seventeenth-century physician and antiquarian Sir Thomas Browne,
he makes a virtue of the idea of style as hot air: one is borne aloft,
he writes, on clauses that rise like warm currents, periods that attain
giddy, eccentric heights of eloquence. Sebald's own prose is similarly
airy, though perhaps, in its strange uniformity, somewhat closer to
the white mist that rises, says Browne, from the bodies of the dead,
'and which during our lifetime ... clouds our brain when asleep or
dreaming'. To try to define Sebald's methods, or track his influence,
can feel somewhat like hoping to bottle such an eerie substance.

*

In February 1884, John Ruskin, then sixty-five years old and already
prey to the mental illness that would later cripple him, delivered
a lecture entitled 'The Storm-Cloud of the Nineteenth Century'.
For over a decade, he claimed, he had been harassed by a malignant
type of cloud: a ghastly, dark and ragged vapour, unprecedented
in the 'traditions of air', and which seemed to the visionary critic
to be composed of dead men's souls. This startling cloud-vision, an
early instance of environmental panic, is also a belated example of
an aesthetic phenomenon that Ruskin had named and deprecated
twenty-eight years earlier. The *pathetic fallacy*, he had written in the
third volume of *Modern Painters*, consisted in the false imputation of
an affective life to a natural object or environment. Only a mind
'unhinged by grief', Ruskin averred, could fall victim to such an error;
a good deal of modern poetry seemed to him to be thus afflicted.

  Sebald was in a sense the ultimate exponent of the
pathetic fallacy: a writer for whom the atmosphere was always in
sympathy with his downcast vision. In this, he took an extraordinary

risk, for the very idea of the atmospheric, let alone its intensification in the pathetic fallacy, could not be less aesthetically respectable. To be seduced by atmosphere, so critical wisdom has it, is to have acceded to mere effect, to have been transfixed by *special effects*, no less. 'Atmosphere' is in any case, one suspects, a naïve name for features of a work of art, or of literary language, that ought more accurately to be described in terms of style, genre, technique and meaning. The atmospheric is a form of deception, a premature sintering of discrete elements into a cloudy, murky, miasmatic whole.

        There is, of course, one genre for which atmosphere is everything, in which air and imagery are inseparable: the Gothic. Recall, for example, the arrival of Edgar Allan Poe's narrator at the appalling House of Usher—the very air is alive, and it is this sentient fog that gives the story its seething tone: 'about the whole mansion and domain there hung an atmosphere peculiar to themselves and their immediate vicinity—an atmosphere which had no affinity with the air of heaven, but which had reeked up from the decayed trees, and the grey wall, and the silent tarn—a pestilent and mystic vapour, dull, sluggish, faintly discernible and leaden-hued.' Sebald sometimes approaches exactly this sort of Gothic excess, though the strangeness of the atmospheric phenomena he asks us to credit may be disguised by the sobriety of his tone. Like Poe, nonetheless, he is a contriver of effects, correspondences and obscure sympathies.

*

In his 1968 book, *Geschmack und Atmosphäre [Taste and Atmosphere]*, Hubertus Tellenbach writes: 'in my experience of our senses there is something more that remains unexpressed. This something more that exceeds the real fact, but that we feel at the same time, we can call the atmospheric.' How to speak of this excess, in literary or artistic terms? How, more precisely, to describe *what is not there*, or at least what cannot be compassed by a description of narrative or style (in the case of literature) or of substance, form and subject (in the case of a work of art, or an exhibition)? It seems that we speak too easily of the 'air' or the 'mood' of an artwork, when in fact it has no mood and breathes, nor gives off, no air. But what if, with Sebald, we were to say that air and atmosphere were essential to our experience of art, that far from giving evidence of inflated abstraction or overly literal affinity, atmospheric excess were precisely what we require of art?

There is an argument to be made that the art of the last century or so is informed—if not exactly dominated—by an obsession with atmospherics. In a literal sense, Marcel Duchamp's vial of *Air de Paris* (1919), Salvador Dalí's appearance at the International Surrealist Exhibition in London in a diving suit and helmet (1936), Andy Warhol's *Silver Clouds* (1966) and Pierre Huyghe's *A Journey That Wasn't* (2006) are all evidence of an abiding artistic interest in air, barometric pressure and the release of certain atmospheres. (An interest mirrored by the gaseous entertainments of the last century—domes, bubbles, all kinds of enclosed and airlocked environments—and shadowed by a more sinister pneumatic history: Zeppelin raids, gas attacks, Zyklon B and the lethal chambers of the US penal system.)

The atmospherics of 'Waterlog'—the mixing of metaphors in that phrase is not unwarranted—are of a more subtle and diffusive sort. Not that that exhibition was afraid of certain Gothic effects: notably, the replica of the skull of Sir Thomas Browne that greeted one on entering and the penumbral half-light into which the whole space had been plunged, as though the exhibition were entombed, or taking place at the bottom of the sea. This last sensation was not entirely fanciful—Alec Finlay's synaesthetic score or 'bell method' recalled the drowned town of Dunwich which, after centuries of erosion and the slow, doomed flight of the town westwards from the coast, has dissolved, as Sebald puts it, 'into water, sand and thin air'. And Guy Moreton's photographs of the Yare and Waveney Valley marshes show landscapes in which each element—air, earth and water—seems to have saturated the others, rendering everything indistinct, letting all landmarks slide towards the horizon, preserving only the atmosphere of the place.

That is not to say, in any sense, that what was visible, or audible, among these works was merely picturesque, nostalgic or melancholic. It was a question, instead, of resuscitation, of an imaginary spirit or afflatus that circulated between the artists, the book and the museum. Immured in a darkened vitrine, eleven dead bitterns from the museum's natural history collection conjured a landscape in which the air was alive with their presence: the rare booming call of the bird, which so fascinated Thomas Browne, resounded in the foyer outside the gallery space. Marcus Coates, whose work appropriated these avian specimens, had composed and sung a song in the local accent: a song that seemed to have been carried on the air from the past, with a warning for the future. Atmosphere, of course, is also a matter of sound, as Alexander and Susan Maris reminded us in *Silentium*: recording a silent landscape precious to Benjamin Britten that was as if haunted in retrospect by the music of Arvo Pärt.

*

If 'Waterlog' was 'inspired' by *The Rings of Saturn*, we ought then to understand *inspiration* in its sense of inflation, of a life or spirit breathed into the works and the space by Sebald's airy volume. It is easy enough to imagine a more literal sort of inspiration: a set of artistic responses and a curatorial approach that simply sought to illustrate or exemplify the writer's subjects and methods. 'Waterlog' instead is a displacement of Sebaldian atmospheres, an indirect application of the logic of association and sympathy that obtains in his books in general, and infuses most thoroughly the pages of *The Rings of Saturn*. The exhibition, in other words, is not a translation of Sebaldian motifs and styles into artistic practice, but a kind of excessive emanation of the book itself, a dissolving of its edges. Or rather, an acknowledgment that Sebald's text has no edges, that its atmosphere leaks away into adjacent landscapes, biographies and histories. In his case, the cliché of the authorial adjective —'Dickensian', 'Beckettian', 'Kafkaesque', to name only three writers obsessed by the effects of enclosed air—becomes a rigorous sort of inspiration. The 'Sebaldian' is less a style than a species of mist through which time and place are transformed.

Applying the adjectives in their least restricted senses— which are in a way the senses that I want to rescue here—Tacita Dean's film *Michael Hamburger* is perhaps the most 'atmospheric' and the most 'Sebaldian' work in the exhibition. The explicit link to *The Rings of Saturn*—a portrait of Sebald's friend, framed in precisely the rooms and garden where the book's narrator discovers him—is only the starting point for a series of static reflections on substance and transformation, air and light, geography and exile. It is a film, in other words, not so much about the incidents and anecdotes that link Hamburger to Sebald, but about the medium in which those connections may be made. Reflecting on his strange sense of having lived Hamburger's life himself, Sebald's narrator asks: 'across what distances in time do the elective affinities and correspondences connect?' Dean asks instead: what is the nature of this light, this shadow, this stillness in a sunlit study or bedroom at dusk, these slight disturbances in the air of early autumn, such that they seem to transport us across those distances?

Surrounded by objects that she might force her subject to make speak of the past, she instead subtilises her gaze and analyses the atmosphere itself for traces of the forgotten, unspoken or unspeakable.

This relay between thing, place and air or mood was effected, as it were, in reverse by Simon Pope's *The Memorial Walks*. What Pope demanded of his walkers was explicitly not a spoken recollection of the style, mood or feeling evoked by the paintings of the Norwich School that he had palled in the manner of a Dutch mourning ritual to which Sebald makes reference at the end of *The Rings of Saturn*. He wanted flat description, a record of trees, buildings, livestock and sky. But accompanying the artist into the countryside around Norwich, standing in the rain before a nondescript stretch of land, one realised that the chosen painting had become nothing more than pure atmosphere: it had been sublimed into the air and become the mere ghost of a painting, its afterglow. Recalling it, hearing your words fail to figure the shadow in your mind's eye, was like trying to clutch at one's own breath.

*

An exhibition is a kind of atmosphere: we find ourselves, for a time, airlocked in the artificial environment that the works and the space conspire to enclose. The organisers of the 1851 Universal Exposition in London, for example, seem to have been keenly aware of the pneumatic nature of the exhibition that took place inside Joseph Paxton's Crystal Palace. It was, noted the catalogue of the exhibition, 'the only building in the world in which the *atmosphere* is perceptible; and the very appropriate style decoration chosen by Mr. Owen Jones greatly adds to the general effect of the edifice. To a spectator situated in the gallery at the eastern or western end, who looks directly before himself, the most distant parts of the building appear enveloped in a bluish halo.' We may think here too of Sebald's description, in *The Rings of Saturn*, of the palm house at Somerleyton Hall, destroyed by a gas explosion in 1913, which had hitherto, he says, shed its gleaming radiance on the dark.

Art, we might venture, is just that realm where the atmosphere becomes visible—except to say that unlike the palace of the glittering commodity or the illuminated pleasure dome (from which, for sure, they are at times inseparable), the museum and the gallery are those spaces where obscurity may become the condition for enlightenment. An atmospheric art—an art, that is, which infolds itself into the dark, which hints at affinities and correspondences across time, which evokes rather than narrates, inspires rather than argues—may well be the art that most closely answers our sense of wonder or curiosity. All knowledge, writes Sebald, echoing Browne, 'is enveloped in darkness. What we perceive are no more than isolated lights in the abyss of ignorance, in the shadow-filled edifice of the world'. But it is the shadows that allow us to see in the first place.

'Waterlog' is in this sense an exhibition about curiosity, about our capacity to drift from one place, one history or one subject to another and still have no notion how we navigated the darkness in between. This is one of Sebald's disorienting skills as a writer: one is constantly turning back to see by what unnoticed sleight he took us, say, from modern Norfolk to seventeenth-century Holland, from the Forbidden City of the 1860s to a darkening view of Berlin in November 1933. The trick is performed in plain view, but seems occulted or shrouded. This is because, as Sebald knows, curiosity does not consist in an eager striving for answers, but is rather the medium in which, by accident or veiled design, we may be cast against subjects we did not even know were there. The exhibition invents a field of knowledge and experience that is irreducible to the mere sum of individual artworks: it conjures up, in other words, an atmosphere.

*

In 1671, the diarist and polymath John Evelyn made his way from London to Norwich, 'having a desire to see that famous scholar and physician Dr. T. Browne'. The two learned men took a tour of the clean and ordered town, Evelyn noting as they went that its flint walls were 'exquisitely headed and squared': which skill, replied Browne, was lost in the mists of time. They visited the cathedral, and walked the 'antique extent of ground' about the Castle, which at that time served as the county gaol. What most impressed the visitor, however, was the domestic museum that his host had amassed: Browne's 'whole house and garden being a paradise and cabinet of rarities, and that of the best collection, especially medals, books, plants, and natural things'. The physician, wrote Evelyn, was particularly taken with the creatures of the air, and had acquired the eggs of all the birds of the region (including, we may surmise, the bittern). His curiosity, like that of the birds themselves, thus extended far beyond the things of this earth, and into the rarefied districts of the atmosphere, where everything rose on columns of air, and was connected.

Marcus Coates

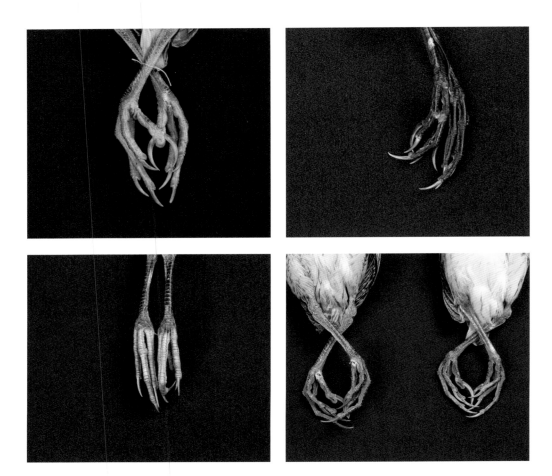

Previous pages and these pages
Britain's Bitterns, circa 1997

Participation has long been an important aspect of Marcus Coates' practice, and in particular the notion of 'becoming animal', that is, taking on an animal's characteristics as either a spiritual journey, or one that imitates basic behaviour. For the exhibition at Norwich Castle Museum and Art Gallery, Coates created two related works, both of which explored the cultural mythology of one of the region's most elusive birds: the bittern.

In a long display case were placed eleven unstuffed bittern specimens—known as 'skins'—from the museum's natural history collection; these represent the total number of males recorded in Britain in 1997, the lowest figure since the 1950s, from which the current population has subsequently grown. Emanating from this rather macabre display, as if from the dead birds themselves, is a song of bitterns and bitterness composed and performed by the artist in local Norfolk dialect and accent, itself a warning—and perhaps example—of man's folly.

The bittern has long been perceived as a messenger of doom, perhaps due to its deep, booming call, a sound that was heard at regular intervals within the rotunda of the Castle Museum. Around this space was also displayed in large text the following quotation from the Old Testament's Book of Zephaniah: 'the bittern shall lodge in the upper lintels of it; their voice shall sing in the windows; desolation shall be in the thresholds.' Given that this warning concerns the Lord's destruction of the city of Nineveh, now known as the Iraqi city of Mosul, the words possessed a distressing contemporary relevance.

Britain's Bitterns circa 1997
Population—11 breeding males
Written and sung by
Marcus Coates

Transcribed into Norfolk dialect
by Colin Burleigh, Friends of
Norfolk Dialect (chairman).

We were born a'fore tha wind
We taught tha reed ter sway
In all tha fen Oi need no friend
Oi 'll hev moi loves ter lay

As Oi wark tha channel edge
Oi 'll feel the sun once more
Wren, water rearl an' reed buntin'
Yew'll sing tha summer raw

Oi live ter stand an' stalk moi prey
Oi am a pearshunt man
Oi weart an' hunt loike this all day
Our way in gods good plan

In all tha warld yew want it new
Yew drearn our land a'plenty
Yew'll hear our call no more, for yew
The east wind will bear empty

Where once tha wet sky covered soil
So dry an' sparse tha reeds now stand
Our fathers proize hare fer their toil
Tha good few hare that are now damned

Yew know us loike yew see tha air
So tell me how long hev we now
So special oh so bludda rare
We'll dew a dance then tearke a bow

Come close an' Oi'll point ter the sky
No more ter yew—Oi'll be the reed
Once caught an' cooked fer tha pie
Now fer tha beets Oi'll sweetly bleed

As Oi stab fish and spare tha frog, woy?
Small sharp mouths must feed
Oi 'd just as well spare yar roight eye
What's left'll see yar greed

Some say it all will end wi' us
Dew Oi knew that Oi'd end it now
No floight or foight or sorry fuss
Jist one more body fer tha plough

Where loys our hope, in yew (sigh) blew sky!
A searlor's jacket p'raps
The sun moight smoile but whoile we die
Yew'll breed that debt no doubts

Oi 'll ne'er leave this moi shrinkin' land
Moine is the deepest croy
Breed an' feed from moi rich hand
Oh come ter me moi loves and doy

George Szirtes

Backwaters: Norfolk Fields
(for W.G. Sebald)

1.

Backwaters. Long grass, Slow speech. Far off
a truck heaves its load of rust into a yard
next to a warehouse full of office furniture
no one will ever use, unless to stuff
some temporary room when times are hard.
Across the fields the sweet smell of manure.

We're years behind. Even our vowels sag
in the cold wind. We have our beauty spots
that people visit and leave alone, down main
arterials and side roads. A paper bag
floats along the beach. Clouds drift in clots
of grey and eventually down comes the rain.

We're at the end. It might simply be of weather
or empire or of something else altogether.

Backwaters: Norfolk Fields (for W.G.

2.

Empire perhaps. Chapels in the cathedral.
Old airstrips. History's human noises
still revving down a field. Clothes pegs hang
like hanged men. It is all procedural.
Resentment simmers in the empty houses.
The wind at its eternal droning harangue.

I'm wanting to mouth the word that fits the case
but it's like trying to roll a shadow from
the street where it has been sitting for years.
It will not go. You cannot wipe the face
of the clock or restore a vanished kingdom.
You feel the shape of the thing between your ears.

Your mouth is talking to the steady light
which listens to you and remains polite.

Sebald)

3.

How beautiful the place is. Watch it hold
time still. I want you to tell me what this is,
this place at the back of beyond, in the sun
that retains its distance in a pale gold
mirror, minding its own brilliant business,
not in the habit of speaking to anyone.

Here is a man who loves cars. He has bought
a house on something very like a hill.
He fills his yard up with old cars. He mends things—
roofs, walls. He's biblical. He does not take thought
for the morrow, won't worry when he falls ill.
He goes swooping along on welded wings,

his children unruly, his wife losing heart.
The beautiful is what keeps them apart.

4.

The WI stall. Jams, flowers. White
hair scraped back in the draught of an open door.
The butcher's. He knows you by name. He calls
your name out. His chopping block is washed bright
by the morning sun. The solicitor
down the street. His nameplate. War memorials

with more names. Rows of Standleys, Bunns,
Myhills, Kerridges. Names on shopfronts: bold
reds, whites and blues in stock typography.
Names on labels tied with string to shotguns.
Names on electoral registers. Names in gold
in the children's section of the cemetery

by the railway cuttings. Willows, faint blue
in the afternoon, light gently whistles through.

5.

Too easy all this, like a fatal charm
intended to lull you into acquiescence.
Think karaoke. Sky. The video shop.
Broken windows. The sheer boredom. The alarm
wailing at two am. The police presence.
Pastoral graffiti on the bus stop.

Think back of the back of beyond 'beyond'. End
of a line. The sheer ravishing beauty
of it as it runs into the cold swell
of the North Sea, impossible to comprehend.
The harsh home truisms of geometry
that flatten to a simple parallel.

This is your otherness where the exotic
appears by a kind of homely conjuring trick.

6.

A fifteen-eighties mural. A hunting scene
runs right around the room. A trace of Rubens,
Jordaens, a touch, even, of Chinese
in the calligraphic lines. Experts clean
the powdery limewash, two PhD students
from the university, anxious to please.

A strange dome appears, out of period
somewhere near the top. Even here
there's something far flung in the code
of a different language, another God
extolling other virtues, a pioneer
morality just waiting to explode.

Flemish brickwork. Devastation. Riders
exploring hidden walls with snails and spiders.

7.

You're out at the end of the pier. It is winter.
Tall waves splutter underfoot. Gulls pirouette
and dive into dark grey. The radio is alive
with music. Its tiny voices seem to splinter
into sharp distinct consonants. You forget
the time of day. It's someone else's narrative

buzzing beneath you. New explorers come
out of the light to exploit the heart of darkness.
The world is inside out, exposed as never before.
Water and sky are a continuum.
A terrible gaiety rustles the sea like a dress
it must discard. It sweeps by just once more

then drops across the beach and remains there
in the memory, in ghosted, mangled air.

8.

How beautiful it is, this silence waiting
on salt. The disused railway lines between
wild blackberries. The faint hum of stray flies
on windowsills. Time is accelerating
down the coast road leaving behind a clean
pair of heels and a whiff of paradise.

The man with welded wings roars past, in love
with reason. His wife leaves in a freak gust,
their children flying along. Dogs race across
the walls in search of a lost treasure trove.
Gently idling, vast trucks deposit rust
in empty yards with patches of dry grass.

Broad fields out of town. The slow unravelling
of a long reel where everyone is travelling.

9.

Travelling through or ending. The damp house
beyond the library where an old woman
has been retreating for some fifty years,
and still retreats towards a dangerous
blind alley, towards a corner, where the nearest demon
might swallow her up leaving no more tears.

There are none left to shed in the overgrown
garden with its coarse weeds. It is as if
she had been sleeping a century or more,
without a retinue, simply on her own,
growing ever more querulous, ever more stiff
till rigor mortis had frozen her four score

into zero. Country aristocracy.
The dead fields at their last-gasp fantasy.

10.

A place full of old women. Hardy, courageous,
muttering to themselves and others in cafés,
engaging unwilling partners in conversation,
accosting young men, making outrageous
advances to middle-aged couples with tea-trays,
embarassing husbands with their ostentation.

Old men in betting shops peering to check
the odds. Old men, natty in white, creaking
over bowls, with Beryl Cook elegance.
Old men tottering, sticking out a neck
at the neighbour while the latter is speaking.
Old men in the church hall learning to dance.

The old in their gerontopolis. At home
in sheltered housing, under the pleasure dome.

11.

How many times do I have to say the word: End!
and still not end. You can't go further than
the sea, not on a motorway. And what
are you doing here, yes, you and your friend
from Morocco, Uganda, St.Kitts or Pakistan?
Whatever has brought you to this far, flat

kingdom with its glum farmers? Surely you
don't think this is America where dreams
are the given, where you swear allegiance
to a new self? Have you somehow fallen through
the net of the world to be lost among reams
of legislature in these alien regions?

Homing. We are homing to the sea. Back
where we never were, at the end of the track.

12.

On a high-cloud day, you could drown in sky
round here. You see the gentle swaying
of leaves along a wall. Something under
the water, under the sky-light, in the dry
cabin under the ocean is quietly playing
a music of muted bells in soft thunder.

It is eating you away until you've gone,
like the spider scurrying up its own spit
back to its natural centre in the dark,
And the sky remains enormous. Someone
is watching the house-martin, the blue tit,
the tiny insects making their tiny mark

in the grass, and the small rain that falls far
across the field as on a distant star.

Tacita Dean

Previous pages
Michael Hamburger
location photograph

These pages
Michael Hamburger
installation photographs

Continuing her ongoing series of film portraits, Tacita Dean's *Michael Hamburger* (2007) is a moving portrayal of the poet and translator, a resident of Middleton and great friend of Sebald, who sadly died in June 2007, a few months after the film was completed.

In its 28 minutes, the film quietly observes the poet in his Suffolk home, its strata of books and papers now somewhat familiar through Sebald's photographs reproduced in *The Rings of Saturn*. The natural and the cultural seep further into one another: sunlight dissolves the frames of the windows, the most insubstantial of thresholds between this home, only one-room-deep, and what lies outdoors; a rainbow marks its watery geometry in the sky; the apples age upon the ground, shrunken, and yet somehow becoming more intensely themselves.

Although Hamburger is said to despair of reviews of his poetry which declare that he is 'better known as a translator', we might detect a similar deprecation of his self, by himself, in the film which shares his name. Unwilling, perhaps unable, to talk of his past and his migrations, most especially fleeing Nazism in 1933, he talks poignantly, instead, of the apple trees in his garden, of where they have come from, and of their careful cross-breeding. Purity is dismissed, and one senses with an awkward pathos that the poet is translating himself.

This page
Michael Hamburger
installation photographs

Opposite page and
following pages
Michael Hamburger
location photographs

fall (for Michael Hamburger)

Alec Finlay

letting go the last of the light of the day the

change what changes change what changes change

the shore with our back to the sea we face

listen only to the winds listen only to the waves listen only to the

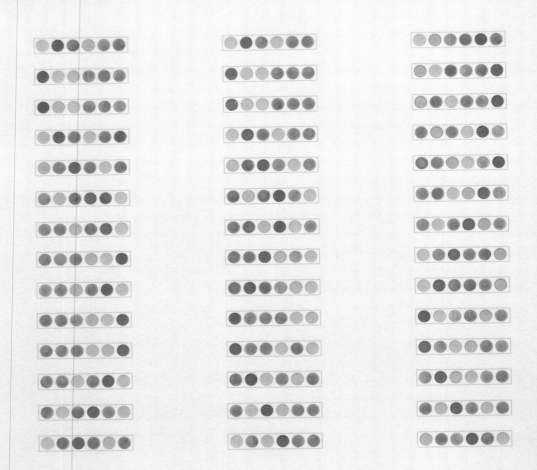

This page
Bell Method (Plain Bob Minor)
detail

Opposite page
Bell Method (Plain Bob Minor)
installation photograph

Walk the shingle at Dunwich, among sea worn stones,
salted pebbles, you'll find amber, or a heart,
like the ones that Gerhard found before us.
He was more discerning about their shapes.

Over the road is the sea, under the waves
the beach; this morning the field floats
swans on a flood of reflected light, where later
out my window a second moon shimmers.

Whatever changes the sea holds the sky's colour;
stars are clear to steer or swim or drown under.
The waves wake the sea's dream; land is ceded;
at All Saints the last grave faces the cliff's edge.

St Bartholomew's, St John's, St Martin's, St Michael's,
all sunk; they say you can hear their bells toll
in the tide. Let's cast a new bell from molten flame,
sink it deep before the sea covers the land.

The Sunken Bell

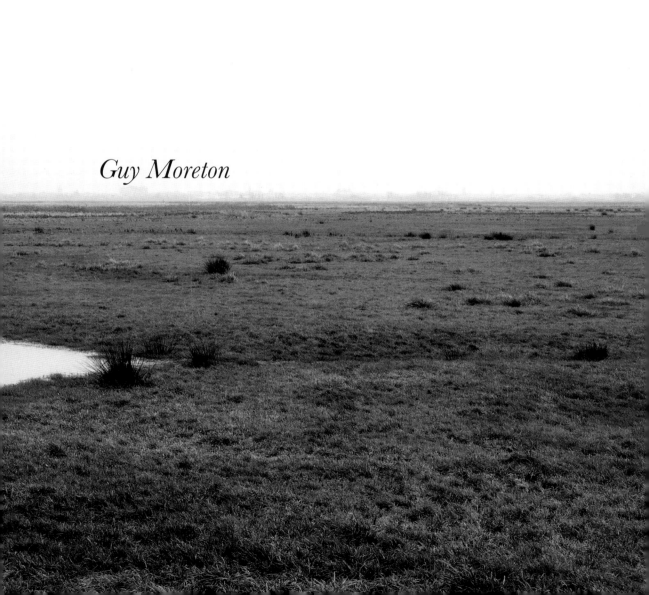

Guy Moreton

Alec Finlay and Guy Moreton's contributions to 'Waterlog' began with a collaborative project called *The Sunken Bell*, which follows the shifting outlines and fluctuating fortunes of the coastline around Dunwich, once one of England's largest ports, and now almost entirely lost to the sea. Inspired by the local legend that on certain tides, bells from Dunwich's many former churches can be heard ringing below the waves, Finlay made a series of thirteen watercolours, transcribing a 'bell method', a score used in church bell ringing. While such methods usually consist of rows of numbers, one for each bell to be rung, Finlay replaces each number with a coloured circle, creating simple pictures with a curiously synaesthetic effect, music having being transformed into colour. The piece reverberated equally affectingly in its transfer to Lincolnshire, along whose coastline, silting as fast as Suffolk's is eroding, the tide deposits material from other places and other times.

Accompanying these paintings were two large-format photographs by Moreton of the ruins of the nearby church of St. Andrew's, Walberswick: vivid reminders of how the certainties of faith and stone are no safeguard against the ravages of time. Leaving these images of this crumbling church tower, the eye alighted on the equally foreshortened edifice of Dunston Pillar, a former 'land lighthouse' built to guide travellers through the dangerous Lincolnshire marshes, now strangely stranded among miles and miles of agricultural land. Shown alongside other photographs by Moreton of the Blyth estuary near Dunwich and of Norfolk's Yare and Waveney marshes, the pillar also stood sentinel over Finlay's companion contributions: circle poems painted on lifebuoys and for inscription on handbells; words that ripple the surface of this otherwise drowned world.

Previous pages
The River Yare 1

These pages
The River Yare 2

Dingle Marsh, Dunwich

Dunston Pillar
detail

East

Matthew Hollis

And if it's permanence you seek
                        then come with me first
to the casting coast—
to the church that lifted its skirts,
slipped through the dunes for the open shore,
before walking into the sea.

Come in calm weather
                          and you'd never know;
but face into an easterly, or a north wind
lifting from Humber, Dogger,
you can sense what once was here.
And now and then, from a scouring storm,
comes the thing itself:
the chancel walls, the drawing wells,
recast on a blasted beach;
or again in what the sea exhumes:
stoneware from Raeren, lintels and pews,
coursed flint, some body bones,
                              or rings;
but never its vows,
the litanies that were swept to sea
and kept there, the many who looked to be one
whose bonds lie broken, taken on the tide
and drowned,
                   so that nothing, no promise, is outliving,
and what's given is given away.

In time, we may refound,
and tell ourselves
we build to build it better. But to walk the strandline,
littered with cuttlebone and uprooted wrack,
is to recognise how little lies within our gift;
how everything else
is in struggle:
the sand sedge clutching for footholds and threads,
the sanderling robbing the tide,
the gabions and groynes shouldering a surge
that cannot begin to be held.
To understand change for what it is,
to go on
when there's nothing to go on,
to be without ordinance and seek only
a temporary stay, to have lived
at the ring-breaker's heel, and lose heavily,
to face despair, and yet
when it comes to the choice,
repair;
because something in the spirit when it rises
does so indomitably:
it is not faith, and not quite hope,
but the ungovernable need to renew.
Whatever you seek
seek here.

Seek solace, mayhem, anything you dare,
but not permanence, nothing abiding.
                                        Or come

and raise your vows against the roar;
say you do, as the thrown winds
hammer and squall,
                                say you will,
as white water fastens and floors,
and the sea comes hunting
a stick man groom,
                                a knot of straw,
a gift of gold to the black-back gulls,
a marram bride
                                in her dress of foam,
her salt heart blistering in its socket.

S. W. FITT NORWICH

REGISTERED

Alexander & Susan Maris

Previous pages
Silentium, film still

These pages
Silentium, film still

If it was observed of Michael Hamburger that, as both poet and translator, he succeeded in placing the best silences in the best order, the same could also be said of the Estonian composer Arvo Pärt, for whom silence is akin to something sacred, and represents the promise of a new beginning. Nowhere is this more explicit than in *Tabula Rasa* (1977), meaning 'blank slate', and in particular its second movement, 'Silentium'.

This contemplative work provides the musical basis, and the title also, of the video *Silentium* (2007) by Alexander and Susan Maris, although they share much more. Indeed if Pärt's composition has been described as possessing the quality of gently swirling mist through which patterns emerge, then the same could be said—perhaps even more accurately—of the Marises' work, in which the sea emerges from an Aldeburgh dawn or our view sweeps slowly across an estuary of invisible silt.

The Marises' chosen locations —the coast at Aldeburgh, upriver towards Snape, and finally Chapel House in Horham—all relate to the life of the English composer Benjamin Britten, whose work was profoundly connected to the region and admired enormously by Pärt. For Britten, Chapel House was a form of sanctuary, a retreat from the overflying USAF planes that disturbed him at his residence, The Red House. In a series of beautifully haunting sequences, the Marises have recreated this quiet escape, retracing this search for silence.

These pages
Silentium, film stills

Following pages
Silentium, film still

Robert Macfarlane

Afterglow, or Sebald Th

Walker

Afterglow, or Sebald The Walker

'Extravagance', Henry David Thoreau noted in *Walden*, means 'to wander excessively'. W.G. Sebald was extravagant in this sense, though in no others. All four of his major works take the form of a walk or walks: through cities, along fraying coastlines, down Alpine valleys.

The category 'walker' has many subdivisions. There are the marathon men: the long-distance land-artist Richard Long, for instance, or Thomas Coryat, who in 1612 marched from London to Agra, and who liked to refer to himself as a *propatetique* (that is, 'a walker forwarde on feete') rather than a *peripatetique* (that is, a person 'who meerely walks arounde'). There are the flaneurs: De Quincey, Defoe, Sean Borodale—anthropologists of the street, botanists of the asphalt, prying their way round cities and towns. There are the psycho-geographers, the downriver dowsers—Iain Sinclair, Chris Petit, Will Self. There are the adventurers—Robert Louis Stevenson, Stephen Graham. And there are the wanderer-wonderers—Samuel Taylor Coleridge, Virginia Woolf.

It is hard, though, to know what to call Sebald: the taxonomy needs stretching. Sinclair recently coined the term 'fugueur', a word whose implicit pugnacity is wrong for Sebald, but whose whisper of 'fugue' does catch at Sebald's strabismic and dream-like pedestrianism. Reading Sebald for the first time, nearly a decade ago, I recalled an entry in Kafka's diary: 'Walked in the streets for two hours, weightless, boneless, bodiless'.

If he was anything, Sebald was a biographer. This is important to understand. He was not a biographer in any conventional sense. He did not erect the flawless porphyry mausolea that Victorian life-writers built about their subjects: tome-tombs. He did not write cradle-to-grave third-person accounts of his subjects, meticulously annotated and documented.

No, Sebald's footnotes were of another kind entirely. For he walked his subjects back into life—or he walked himself forwards into death (it can be hard to tell which). He travelled the routes formerly taken by his subjects, visited the sites they did. He tried to see something of what they might have seen (I think here of that chilling image of the bright train-tracks near the start of *The Emigrants*—a version of Paul Bereyter's last view on earth). In this way, memories, visions, revealed themselves to Sebald: glimpses of lives lived, deaths died. And the representation of these walks, these glimpses, constituted Sebald's biographical art (failed, incomplete): his account of the no-longer-living. Some of his biographees were famous—Kafka, Chateaubriand, Fitzgerald. Others were not: Paul Bereyter, Ambros Adelwarth, Dr Henry Selwyn. All of them were men.

That Sebald should have been a walker, a traverser of ground, was of course appropriate to his subjects. For each was in some way displaced, either from himself, his family, or his heartland. Refugees, melancholics, wanderers... Sebald wrote about the territorially and emotionally dispossessed—those who had been forced on treks and flights into exile.

And to an exile, as Christopher Gregory-Guider has nicely observed, 'place' means 'the sum total of all the locations that have been left behind.' Walking was therefore a fitting way for Sebald to search for his peripatetic subjects. I say 'search for', because he never encounters his subjects. He only ever registers the evidence of their previous presences—marks of the once-was or the has-been. He records a tracery-work of the vanished.

Sebald's work is filled with beautiful images for this tracery-work. The dust that floats through his writing, for example, or the ash that settles on its surfaces—these are the substances of residue, of vestige. And there is also the starlight, the strange sidereal lustre that illuminates so much of his prose. Starlight, when it arrives on earth, is the evidence of ancient astral events, occurring many light years previously: former combustions, long-finished collapses.

My favourite of these images occurs early in Sebald's last book (itself a trace of the vanished). Austerlitz is recalling a childhood summer night in North Wales, when he and his Great Uncle Alphonso walked at dusk up onto a hill above the Mawddach Estuary, carrying an 'incandescent lamp'. Once full dark falls, Alphonso places the lamp in a shallow hollow of heather, and lights it. Immediately, moths start to fly at them: thousands upon thousands of moths, drawn to the lamp's halo. After a few minutes of this soft barrage, Austerlitz realises that he is not able to see the moths themselves—so quickly do they move through the lamp's halo—but only the light flares they incite. The 'trails of light which [the moths] seemed to leave behind them,' Austerlitz says:

in all kinds of curlicues and streamers and spirals ... did not really exist, but were merely phantom traces created by the sluggish reaction of the human eye, appearing to see a certain afterglow in the place from which the insect itself, shining for only the fraction of a second in the lamplight, had already gone.

‘Afterglow’: the German word is ‘*Nachglanz*’, a beautiful coinage original to Sebald. It has echoes of another neologism, *Abglanz*, which Goethe uses in Faust, and which carries Platonic implications of ‘reflection’, ‘mirror image’—the world being only an ‘Abglanz’ of another, truer version. Doubly, then, Sebald’s *Nachglanz* is a word that describes a vision of absence. The quick-vanishing moths, with their ashy wings, exist only as retinal ghosts, hovering at the limits of both the visual and the representational.

Walking was a kind of mothing for Sebald: a way to draw out the afterglow of the ‘already gone’. Virginia Woolf wrote excitedly of experiencing ‘an incessant shower of innumerable atoms’. She lived acutely in the present, as did her prose. Sebald and his characters live acutely in the past: they move through a light-storm of afterglow.

~

What does it mean to haunt a haunter, to footstep a footstepper? For several months now, I have been following Sebald—and I will continue to follow him for two or more years to come. I have started to re-make certain of the walks that Sebald (or his narrators) take in each of the main four books: the walk down into Wertach im Allgau from the Oberjoch Customs Point (*Vertigo*); the walk down off the Dark Peak and into the docklands of Manchester (*The Emigrants*); the walk south along the Suffolk coast (*The Rings of Saturn*); and a series of London walks, between cemeteries and churches (*Austerlitz*). I am turning Sebald’s own methods back onto him: walking where he walked, seeing what emerges, what ‘phantom traces’ or afterglow Sebald himself left.

There are precedents for such behaviour. Janet Malcolm chased Chekhov. Robert Dessaix followed Turgenev. Iain Sinclair tracked John Clare’s flight out of Essex. Geoff Dyer struggled with D.H. Lawrence. Robert Smithson has been variously pursued by at least two of the other contributors to the present publication. For all these followers, walking makes for content, footage for footage. For several, it becomes something more mystical. This method of biography was pioneered by Richard Holmes in the 1980s, who tracked Robert Louis Stevenson, Shelley and Coleridge among others. Biography, Holmes wrote 'was ... a kind of pursuit, a tracking of the physical trail of someone's path through the past, a following of footsteps. You would never catch them; no, you would never quite catch them.' I have not set out to catch Sebald, for I have no belief that such capture is possible or valuable.

What have I discovered so far? Two things. First, that Sebald's route is littered with false turnings, decoys and red herrings. An example: in *The Emigrants*, the Sebald-like narrator describes how, on arrival in East Anglia in the mid-1970s, he and his wife moved into a decaying country house 'in the village of Hingham'. When I visited the poet George Szirtes in Wymondham, to talk with him about Sebald, I mentioned this detail. 'No,' Szirtes said, 'this is wrong. The house Sebald lived in when he first arrived is only a few yards from here. Hingham is in fact Wymondham.' This was my first lesson in Sebald's space-shuffling. 'Hingham is in fact Wymondham.' I have written this on a small piece of paper and tacked it to a shelf above my desk: a motto for my journeys.

The other thing I have learnt is that, following Sebald, strange things occur. Two examples of this. The first—not my own—concerns the artist Jeremy Millar, who in 2006 travelled to the point on the A146 near Norfolk where Sebald was killed in a car-crash. On the roadside, Millar lit a firework, and took photographs of the smoke plume left behind by the rocket. Extraordinarily, in one photograph the smoke has formed into a spectral image of Sebald's own distinctive, moustached face.

The other example. In May of this year, I was out at Shingle Street in Suffolk, following Sebald's route down that coast. I walked along the tideline—the sea rough and brown to my east, the shingle hissing and sliding beneath my feet—for half a mile or so, and then climbed a steep gravel berm back up onto the main beach. And there, unexpectedly, was a shell-line. It was made of rock whelks, thousands upon thousands of them, their shells bleached bright white, laid side by side. Fifty or so shells to the yard, and the line ran for hundreds of yards: meandering away from me, dipping and rising over the shingle dunes, inland and out of sight. It began at no particular point—simply emerged, like a river surfacing after miles underground. Where it met a clump of sea cabbage or sea kale, it split into two, passed to either side of the clump, then re-braided again. Who had made it? And why? But neither question, I realised, was of interest or value. The line had been made, and was beautiful, and its gratuity was its point. It was innocent, childish and freely given. I turned aside from my Sebaldian route, and followed the line inland, to see where it led.

I have come to think of Sebald's work, and my work on Sebald, as versions of revision: both in the sense of re-seeing and re-writing. Henry James once connected revision and walking. Describing the process of revising his own prose, he used the metaphor of tracking an earlier self through winter country. 'It was,' James said:

as if the clear matter being still there, even as a shining expanse of snow spread over a plain, my exploring tread, for application to it, had quite unlearned the old pace and found itself naturally falling into another, which might sometimes indeed more or less agree with the original tracks, but might most often, or very nearly, break the surface in other places. What was thus predominantly interesting to note, at all events, was the high spontaneity of these deviations and differences.

It is an exquisite and unexpected meditation on rewriting, which— as we would expect from James—practices what it describes. Thus we hear the subtle revision of 'pace' into 'place', for instance, as well as the deviation from the expected in that last phrase: not a 'high frequency of deviations and differences', but a 'high spontaneity'.

Most interesting to me, though, is James's sense of how following the footsteps of a previous traveller might lead one not to replicate but to innovate. How, in his phrasing, 'trying to walk' in 'original tracks' might in fact lead one to 'break the surface in other places'. This was what happened to Sebald, and I hope it will happen to me.

Simon Pope

The east stands for lost causes, Sebald wrote in *The Rings of Saturn*, and of those things lost, to which he refers, perhaps the greatest is the vast expanse of woodland which grew upon the flatlands of East Anglia before being destroyed by settlers and avaricious landowners. Often, such woodland now exists only in the art of the region, most especially the paintings of the Norwich School, the first provincial art movement in Britain, and the inspiration behind Simon Pope's *The Memorial Walks* (2007). In this project, an invited participant chooses a painting, from either the Norwich or the Lincoln collections, that portrays trees or woodland in particular, and then memorises it; they must then walk to a location of Pope's choosing—generally within striking distance of the gallery—before then describing the picture from memory, a process of recollection which is recorded on tape and photographed. The process is repeated for each painting.

The paintings themselves are hung within the gallery, although most are draped with black silk, reminiscent of the ancient Dutch ritual practised in homes in which there had been a death, whereby landscape paintings and mirrors were draped with mourning ribbons in order that the departing soul would not become distracted upon its final journey. At regular intervals during the exhibition, a different painting was unveiled, and its recalled description made available (as an audio file) on the 'Waterlog' website; the other paintings were left to reside in our memories, or our imaginations.

Previous pages
from The Memorial Walks

These pages
The Memorial Walks

These pages
from The Memorial Walks

Following pages
The Memorial Walks

Colman Collection

Tacita Dean

W.G. Sebald

Map found by Joseph Dean
in Goch, 1944.
Photo: J. Littkemann

Right
Found photographs of Goch, 1944.

Far right
Goch, 2003.
Photos: Dr. Georg Kersting

At Christmas two years ago, I was given a reproduction silk map of the city of Berlin. Seeing the map triggered a memory for my father. He was a Captain in the 51st Highland Division as it moved slowly through Holland into Germany in the Allied advance late in 1944. He remembers seeing a flat expanse of land bordering the river, across which, he recounts, his four guns had just fired a small high explosive barrage as part of an air landing exercise on the other bank. They watched the planes flying over, and when they came back, he saw that one of them was smoking and, to his horror, losing height and heading straight towards him. He couldn't bear to see it crash, so ducked into his slit trench. The plane crashed into muddy soil about a hundred yards away, and when he walked over, the only recognisable object was an envelope lying on the ground marked 'map'.

And then my father went upstairs and returned, remarkably quickly, with the map he had kept for 57 years, which he gave to me. The envelope was made of what felt like rubberised cotton and had the words, 'MAPS ONLY' printed on the front. Inside was a large folded silk map of Germany and its border with Holland and France. They were made for pilots from the Royal Air Force, and

Photographs of the bombing of
Goch, taken from the Steenbeck
of the film, *Krieg am Niederrhein*
by Heinz Bosch and Wilhelm Haas,
1981.
Courtesy Imperial War Museum
and Kreis Kleve

printed on silk so as not disintegrate in water. We opened up the map,
poignantly unused, and my father tried to find the place where he had
found it. 'There', he pointed a tiny dot, 'there: I found it in Goch.'

I was in Amsterdam for the palindrome date of 20. 02. 2002. The
following morning, I caught an early train to Arnhem, where I was
picked up at the station by Rita Kersting, Director of the Kunstverein
in Düsseldorf, the gallery where I was going to have a show later
in the year. We drove to the Kröller-Müller Museum in Otterlo.
It was a clear February day, and everything felt tamed and safe and
comfortable as Holland often does. We went to see the exhibition of
Dan Graham, and afterwards drove back through the wooded
parkland heading for Düsseldorf.

Somewhere near Nijmegen, we got lost trying to find
the autobahn. We drove in the dusk around and around in those
lands straddling the border: strange petrol stations, new woods and
neat housing. We didn't know which country we were in. Rita told
me that she came from a town also quite near to the Dutch border,
which was so small I would not have heard of it. I don't know what
it was about that landscape and that place, and the atmosphere of
that moment, which made me ask, quite suddenly, if she came
from Goch?

So then we went to Goch, one evening later in the year,
to have dinner with Rita's parents, both doctors now retired. Their
house had been their practice, so intervening doors were now being
permanently sealed up, and those years of service to the community
of Goch, put away. Rita's father, Georg, was evacuated to Ossendorf
on December 6th 1944 when Goch was declared a red zone. He was
ten years old. When he returned nine months later in September 1945,
his town was ruined. His most enduring memory was of walking in
through the normal door of the church and looking up at the ceiling,
and there being nothing there but sky. The steeple had been used as
a lookout, and was blown up not by the Allies, it seems, but by the
retreating Germans fearing its appropriation. He remembers being
most shocked by a display of photographs in a shop window taken
by British war journalists that were for sale. It was only then that he
saw the piles of rubble in the market place, and the unrecognisable
state of his hometown.

Tacita Dean in the bus stop,
Naselesele, Fiji.
Photo: Mathew Hale

W.G. Sebald wrote, in an article published in *The New Yorker* after his death in 2001, about the very strange place the bombing of German cities has in the collective memory of the people. He writes not only of the extraordinary efficiency and speed with which the rubble was cleared and reconstruction begun, but also of the protective amnesia that settled in after the air raids finally ended. As if, he writes, 'the images of this horrifying chapter of our history have never really crossed the threshold of the national consciousness.' Most documented observations, he continues, were made by foreign journalists and writers, repulsed at the damage inflicted by them on a civilian population, whereas in Germany itself, there was near silence.

In September 1999, I was in Fiji recording 24 hours of continuous sound in the bus shelter of the village of Naselesele, Taveuni Island. The sound, wild sound of a particular place with a longitude of 180°, was for a project situated outside the much-unloved Millennium Dome in London. I sat in the bus shelter, with my digital recorder next to me,

reading W.G. Sebald's *The Rings of Saturn*. I remember the situation well because I remember what I read. I remember the village in front of me—houses spread out on a grass incline covered with small flowering trees, and the hundreds of children whose excited voices I recorded. It had rained the night before and everything was vivid, and I started to read about Roger Casement.

I had first learnt about Roger Casement from Katy English. I was staying with her in their house in Cushendun, County Antrim—a wonderful old-fashioned place where I often went in the autumn. We were sitting in the drawing room one afternoon, where, Katy told me, Roger Casement would often come to tea with the house's former occupant, Ada McNeill. Ada McNeill lived at Glendun Lodge on grace and favour from her brother Lord Cushendun. She was a woodcarver, and a keen walker who carried a gun wherever she went, shooting up into the sky to scare off boys scrumping for apples. She was also a fervent nationalist, and held quite a candle for Roger Casement, although her sexuality was as undiscussed as his own.

She is even rumoured to have buried guns for him in her garden.

Roger Casement's Protestant father and Catholic mother died when he was still quite young, so he was brought up by his aunt and would often stay with his relatives in County Antrim; he also attended the Ballymena Academy. The Casement family land was, and still is, near by Cushendun in the direction of Ballycastle, and his favourite ever place, he wrote to his cousin Gertrude Bannister from Pentonville prison, was the old church ruin of Drumnakill looking over Murlough Bay. Some historians believe it to be the site of the thirteenth station of the cross on an ancient pilgrim walk, and it is here that a memorial was built to Roger Casement, which has been so badly vandalised that all that remains of it today is a concrete base and a metal prong.

So I read in my bus stop idyll about Casement's meeting with Joseph Conrad, which so impressed the latter that he believed he was the only man of integrity he had met amongst all the Europeans in the Congo. And I read about the report that Casement delivered to the British Foreign Service on the atrocities committed at the hands of the white imperialist enterprise on the black labour force that was such a shocking revelation it forced Belgium to reassess its colonial strategies.

Postcard from Murlough Bay,
Co. Antrim.
© Ulster Card Company Ltd

And then I read about Casement's involvement in the struggle for an
independent Ireland...

The facts are well known: with the outbreak of the First
World War, both the Ulster Volunteer Force and the Irish Volunteers
were instructed to join up and fight for Britain against Germany.
There was great disillusion amongst the Volunteers who refused to
fight for a nation that was, in their opinion, actively oppressing
Irish Nationalism. So a breakaway group was formed, and a plan
was hatched to ask the Germans for support in their fight for Home
Rule and an envoy was dispatched to secure arms. That envoy was
Roger Casement.

Sebald writes with great tenderness about Roger
Casement: the exhausted man, far too old and unwell to be wading
through icy water, who was dropped off by a German submarine
on the southwest coast of Ireland after having failed his mission.
He had only managed to acquire one tenth of what he had asked
for, and had just time to send a message to Dublin to try and call off
the uprising, which, in the end, no one heeded. He was too weak to
run away, and took refuge in McKenna's Fort where he was found
by a local Constable and arrested. The boat carrying the arms,
Aud Norge, disguised as a Norwegian merchant ship, waited off the
coast of County Kerry for land signals, but none came. Eventually, it
was intercepted by the Royal Navy and told to head for Cork. And,
as pre-arranged in such a circumstance, the crew put back on their
German naval uniforms, raised their flag and surrendered, scuttling
the boat as they did so, and detonating the charges off Daunt's Rock.

At his trial at the Old Bailey, Casement acted for his own
defence and, according to Sebald , the Counsel for the prosecution was
the very man, Frederick Smith, who had led the Ulster Protestants

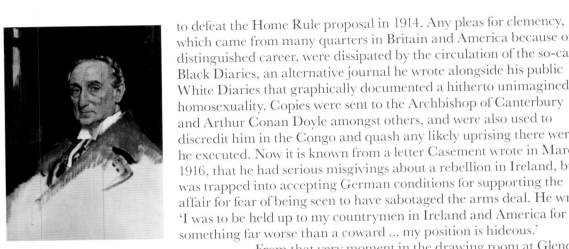

Rufus Isaacs, 1st Marquess of Reading, painting by William Orpen, 1919.
Courtesy National Portrait Gallery, London

to defeat the Home Rule proposal in 1914. Any pleas for clemency, which came from many quarters in Britain and America because of his distinguished career, were dissipated by the circulation of the so-called Black Diaries, an alternative journal he wrote alongside his public White Diaries that graphically documented a hitherto unimagined homosexuality. Copies were sent to the Archbishop of Canterbury and Arthur Conan Doyle amongst others, and were also used to discredit him in the Congo and quash any likely uprising there were he executed. Now it is known from a letter Casement wrote in March 1916, that he had serious misgivings about a rebellion in Ireland, but was trapped into accepting German conditions for supporting the affair for fear of being seen to have sabotaged the arms deal. He wrote, 'I was to be held up to my countrymen in Ireland and America for something far worse than a coward ... my position is hideous.'

From that very moment in the drawing room at Glendun Lodge, when I first heard account of Roger Casement's life, I found it very difficult to reconcile the conflicting truths in his story. Yet I am very attracted to him as an historical figure, and even though I can see the obvious treason to the British government of landing in a German submarine off the coast of Ireland during the First World War, I wish he had not been executed in the climate he was: where no account was given for what he had achieved in Africa, and where all those who supported and respected him were hushed into a conspiratorial homophobia. And so it was that I learnt, as I read Sebald's moving chapter in the bus shelter in Fiji, that the presiding judge who put on the black cap for Roger Casement, and uttered those terrifying words that I can hardly bear to write:—'You will be taken hence to a lawful prison and thence to a place of execution and will be there hanged by the neck until you be dead...'—was my great, great uncle, Sir Rufus Isaacs.

There were nine children born to the union of Sara Davis and Joseph Isaacs. Rufus was the fourth: Frances, Nelly and Harry were older, and Albert, Florence, Godfrey, Frederick and Esther were younger. Florence was my great, great grandmother.

The family tree, which my uncle produced for me, is a beautiful document on several sheets of folded paper, neatly inscribed in his hand. On the top left side is 'Isaac (? in Germany)', and on the top right is 'Aron Mendoza—Ritual Slaughterer—c. 1725'. Aron was a Sephardic Jew from Portugal, who wrote a book in Hebrew about prize fighting. Both his son and grandson seemed to have carried on the family profession, while his daughter, named Pyra 'exorcised evil spirits' as her trade. The tree spreads out: still on the right hand side, I trace the lines down to Aron's prize fighting grandson, Daniel, who had eleven children of his own, one of whom, Welcome Mendoza, was grandmother to one Peter Sellers '(actor)'. On the left hand side, I read that Isaac (? in Germany)'s son Michael settled at Chelmsford in England at some point at the beginning of the eighteenth century. The two sides meet eventually some hundred years later, on the fold of the paper, with the marriage of Sara Mendoza to Michael Isaacs '(fruit brother)' who were grandparents to Rufus and his siblings.

From what I can tell, the Isaacs were a close-knit family. Joseph Isaacs was a fruit merchant like his father, and his eldest son, Harry, later took over the business. Rufus trained as a lawyer and entered Parliament as a Liberal in 1904, becoming Attorney General in 1910. His brother, Godfrey, became Managing Director of the Marconi Telegraph Company, both in Britain and America. Esther and Florence studied painting together in Paris at the height of Impressionism, and we still have some of Esther's paintings on the walls at home.

In 1912, Rufus and Godfrey were both involved in The Marconi Scandal. The Liberal Government, under Herbert Asquith, had approved of a plan to erect a series of wireless stations around the British Empire, and the contract was put out to tender. A year later, it was agreed to offer the work to the Marconi Telegraph Company. During that winter, articles started to appear in the press, most notably in the political weekly, *The Eye Witness* by such writers as Cecil Chesterton and Hilaire Belloc, clearly implying that Rufus Isaacs, Lloyd George and other members of the Cabinet had profited from insider knowledge about the contract.

Both brothers sued for libel and won. Rufus against a French newspaper, which openly accused him and the Postmaster General, H.L. Samuel, of corruption, and Godfrey against Cecil Chesterton. The cases brought the issue to public attention, and in 1913, Rufus Isaacs and Lloyd George were asked to make statements to a Committee explaining their actions. It appeared that Rufus had in fact bought ten thousand Marconi shares from another brother, Harry Isaacs, but they were from the American company, not the British

one. He, in turn, sold a portion of them to Lloyd George, Samuels and
the Chief Liberal Whip, Lord Murray, who even acquired some for
the Liberal Party. The Ministers stated to the Committee that as the
American Company would not benefit directly from the contract, they
believed it to be an entirely private transaction.

In June 1913, it was decided that charges of gross
corruption were unfounded, but that the Ministers had been ill advised
in buying the shares and delaying the disclosure of the facts. No blame
was awarded to anyone except to those who had circulated the charges
of corruption. However, the vote was not unanimous. The Unionist
members held that the Ministers had acted with grave impropriety,
and forced the issue into a debate in the House of Commons. Rufus
Isaacs and Lloyd George, while protesting good faith, admitted
their error of judgement, and a motion was passed accepting their
statements by 346 votes to 268.

When I asked my father about the affair, he told me
that Rufus had always maintained to his sister Florence that the
reason he had been less than candid about the shares was that he was
advised to be so by Lloyd George. Whatever the story, the scandal did
unleash a wave of anti-Semitism, particularly addressed at the Jewish
'ringleaders' of the affair: Rufus, Godfrey and H.L. Samuel. This
reached its most insidious point with the publication of a vicious hate
poem by Rudyard Kipling called, 'Gehazi', directly addressing Rufus's
subsequent promotion to Lord Chief Justice in 1913, comparing him to

the rapacious and cunning Biblical character, Gehazi who was cursed with leprosy for betraying his master. The poem ends:

> What means the risen whiteness,
> Of the skin between thy brows?
> The boils that shine and burrow,
> The sores that slough and bleed –
> The leprosy of Naaman
> On thee and all thy seed?
> Stand up, stand up, Gehazi,
> Draw close thy robe and go,
> Gehazi, Judge in Israel,
> A leper white as snow!

Gugliemo Marconi supported his Managing Director throughout the Marconi Scandal; they seem to have been very close colleagues. When Godfrey died, just months after retiring from the company due to ill health and overwork, Marconi's letter of condolence to his widow is so scored out as to appear grief stricken. When he took over the position in 1910, Godfrey was zealous in his enforcement of the company's patents, which gave him the reputation of being a litigious man, but evidently his energy, business intelligence, and enthusiasm for the new science, coupled with Marconi's inventive brilliance, were fundamental in establishing wireless communication in Britain.

Marconi was born in Bologna, but his mother was Irish. Inspired by the discovery that electromagnetic waves exist in the air, he began experimenting, and lodged the first patent for 'wireless technology' in 1896. Two years later, Lloyds of London invited him to experiment with overseas wireless links over the small stretch of water between Ballycastle and Rathlin Island in County Antrim. Marconi sent his assistant, George Kemp, who after various trials managed to receive the first radio signal ever transmitted over sea. As it happened, it was across the very bay that Roger Casement found so dear and which is overlooked today by his broken monument. Also, ironically, it is where *U-19*, the very same German submarine which had brought Casement home two years before, torpedoed and sank the armed merchant cruiser, *HMS Calgarian* with the loss of 49 lives.

Guglielmo Marconi with Godfrey Isaacs attending the court enquiry into the disaster of the sinking of the *Titanic*, 1912.
© Marconi Corporation plc

It was evidently a particular concern of Marconi's to end isolation at sea, and one of his first moves with the advancement of his technology was to put radio operators on board ships. These men were often radio enthusiasts and were employed, not by the shipping companies, but by Marconi himself. It was an expensive business that used a lot of electricity with long aerials strung up the ship's masts. Weather conditions dictated how far a signal could travel, and it was often easier to work at night. Initially, the technology seems to have been much more attractive to First Class passengers with money to spend on sending greetings to those at home, than to captains accustomed to silence at sea. Messages would hopscotch from boat to boat until they reached land. It was also fairly common not to signal to boats using rival technology, namely not the Marconi brand. Business competition at sea was rife.

All this is what went wrong, as well as right, on the evening of April 14th 1912 when *Titanic* hit an iceberg somewhere in the north Atlantic. Radio operator, Harold Bride seems to have prioritised sending the passengers' messages over an incoming ice warning from another ship, the *Californian*. There was no direct communication to the bridge, so subsequent ice warnings were not passed on. However, after the collision, he did manage to get a distress warning to three ships including the *Carpathia*, which arrived in time to save 700 lives, but the operator of the *Californian*, the closest ship by over a hundred miles, had already gone to bed.

At the enquiry into the *Titanic* disaster, presided over by Rufus Isaacs, who was still the Attorney General at that time, Marconi wireless technology was pronounced the saver of many lives. Twenty-four hour wireless watch became mandatory at sea and the

Intérieur du Café Carrel, Arles by
Vincent Van Gogh, Arles, August
1888. Oil on canvas.
Courtesy of James Roundell, London

price of Marconi shares rapidly appreciated. But such a commentator
and seamen as Joseph Conrad could only look cynically upon such a
misadventure, as he wrote in 1912 in his observation, *Some reflections,
Seaman-like and otherwise, on the loss of the Titanic*:

> ... to the applause of two continents, you launch that
> mass with 2,000 people on board at 21 knots across the
> sea—a perfect exhibition of the modern blind trust in
> mere material and appliances ... if that luckless ship had
> a couple of feet shorter, she would probably have gone
> clear of the danger. But then, perhaps, she could not
> have had a swimming bath and a French café: a sort of
> marine Ritz, proclaimed unsinkable and sent adrift with
> its casual population upon the sea, without enough boats,
> without enough seamen...

My father and uncle both have memories of Rufus, a kindly but sharply intelligent old man, who was much happier after his second marriage to his secretary, Stella Charnaud. He was made Viceroy of India at the time when Gandhi was gaining prominence in 1921, and then returned to be Foreign Secretary in Ramsay MacDonald's 1931 National coalition government.

His sister Florence married a business acquaintance of her brother Harry's in the fruit trade, who was always called Tommy in the family but born Albert Van Gruisen. His father was a Dutchman, and grandson of the famous Friesland organ builder, Albertus Van Gruisen; his mother was English. They were my great, great grandparents.

Their youngest sister Esther married the playwright Alfred Sutro but they had no children. In 1896, while on a trip to Paris, Esther bought from the Ambroise Vollard Gallery in Rue Lafitte a painting by Vincent Van Gogh. The painting was called, *Intérieur du Café Carrel, Arles* which he had painted in 1888, just two years before he died. She became its first owner, and brought the painting back to England where it hung in her home at Chester Terrace. My father remembers the painting as a large oil scene 'with those restaurant chairs he painted so often'. Great-aunt Essie, as she was known to him, died intestate in 1934 and the painting was passed on briefly to her sister Florence Van Gruisen. She sold it in 1935, much to the perpetual regret of the family, for about £2,500, and divided the proceeds amongst the remaining Isaacs siblings.

I decided to track it down, and looked through all his paintings for scenes that matched my father's childhood memory. Only when I took to the Internet and typed in 'Goch' instead of 'Gogh' did it occur to me that his family might well have come from the German town at the heart of this narrative. In the introduction to the 1953 edition of *The Collected Letters of Vincent Van Gogh*, his sister-in-law, Jo van Gogh-Bonger confirms this by explaining that the family name 'Van Gogh' derives from the small German town on the Dutch border, and that it is a name which has existed since the sixteenth century.

In my search for the painting, I came up with three options: three restaurant interiors, one painted in Paris and two in Arles. The Parisian scene was in the collection of the Kröller-Müller Museum. Could we have inadvertently looked upon Esther's Van

Gogh that afternoon in February? In the end, I discovered through its provenance, that it was one of the other two Arles paintings, and that its current whereabouts appeared clouded in a great and mysterious secrecy, which has taken the help of several experts to unravel.

It was sold in 1935 through the Lefevre Gallery to America where it stayed in Providence, Rhode Island until it appeared at a Christie's auction in 1996. It was then sold once more for over ten million dollars to a London dealer, who was formerly the Christie's specialist on Impressionism. Who they sold it to after that, when, and for how much was of the utmost sensitivity, I was told. And only yesterday, on the eve of finishing this text, did I learn that *Intérieur du Café Carrel, Arles* is back in America and currently somewhere in Texas, apparently promised one day to the Kimbell Art Museum in Fort Worth.

So that February evening, we found our way onto the autobahn, and arrived in Düsseldorf well after dark. I learnt later, the city had invited Sebald to receive the Heinrich Heine award, exactly a year and a day before he was killed in a car accident in Norfolk on 14 December 2001. In photographs, taken that day by the town hall, Sebald looks awkward and wary of such civic formalities, as he uncomfortably holds open, with the help of the mayor, the oversized book displaying the laudation; the flash having bleached out any details written inside it.

The Presentation of the Heine
Prize to W.G. Sebald in the Senate
Room of County Hall in the City of
Düsseldorf by the Mayor Joachim
Erwin on December 13th, 2000.
Photo: Wilfried Meyer

*Postscript**

Just over three weeks ago, I drove to London from Berlin on my way to
Kent. I woke up that first morning to hear on the radio that a painting
of the Appeal of Roger Casement was due to go on show to the public
the following day in the National Portrait Gallery. It was a news event.
I was surprised as one of my starting points in the writing of 'W.G.
Sebald' had been to try and locate a drawing of Casement which had
once appeared in a newspaper and which I'd had pinned up above my
desk for some time. My research had started in the National Portrait
Gallery where it appeared they only had two awkward pencil drawings
by Sir William Rothenstein in their collection, drawn in 1911 around
the time of Casement's knighthood.

So I went in that afternoon to look at *High Treason, Court
of Criminal Appeal 1916: The Trial of Roger Casement* painted by John
Lavery. It was a large painting, recently cleaned—the action strangely
inert and dull. The painter had been sitting in the empty jury box
opposite and facing Casement, who sat alone looking back. Everyone
else is uncomfortably foreshortened and squashed into the picture
plane. They are preoccupied, and in profile, as they focus on the Bench
to the left of the painting. Only one other person, I noticed, had her
face turned towards the painter. She too is looking out, but her eyes
are not defiant like those of Casement, but slightly downcast. I looked
at the crude key to identify her, and was taken aback to see that it was
Ada McNeill.

It was the presiding Appeal Judge, a Unionist supporter
named Darling, who had personally commissioned the painting.
A friend of the artist, he had invited Lavery to document his role in
an event he believed would be the most important state trial of the
century. Not a stranger to vanity, he had already had himself depicted
once before by Lavery in full judicial robes and black cap, pronouncing
a death sentence. That painting was thought by many to be in bad
taste, and the Casement one also attracted criticism, which might be
the reason why it was never finished at the time, and ended up still
in Lavery's possession. It was bequeathed on his death in 1941 to the
National Portrait Gallery but was declined, although it was kept there
until the end of the War. It was then offered to the Royal Courts of
Justice who accepted it, with some embarrassment, and was eventually

hung in 1947 out of public view in a room occupied by the Clerk to the Registrar of Criminal Appeals.

In 1950, Serjeant Sullivan, who had been Counsel for the defence in Casement's Appeal (depicted addressing the Court to the right of the painting), wrote to the Lord Chancellor to ask if he could acquire the painting for the King's Inns in Dublin. It was decided that it was better to loan it, or as the Lord Chief Justice put it: 'We can adopt the suggestion of lending it to the King's Inns on indefinite loan which means we can forget to ask for its return.' Sullivan accepted, replying: 'Since even the profession have consigned the picture to gloom and forgetfulness for thirty years, I do not anticipate any new awakening to its charm. If such yearning shall seize the British Public they shall have it back. May you live and flourish as I would wish till then.'

Berlin, July, 2003

*For his help in writing the postscript, I would like to thank John McBratney, Honorary Secretary of King's Inns, Dublin. He was hitherto unknown to me, but he happened to ring up Dorothy Cross as I sat with her on her lawn in Tully Cross, Connemara, where I had gone to stay on the second leg of the trip. He was excited to tell her he'd just been to London for the official unveiling (a small gathering of sixteen people) of *High Treason, Court of Criminal Appeal 1916: The Trial of Roger Casement* in the National Portrait Gallery: the very event I'd heard discussed on the radio my first morning in London.

'Who is this who is coming?'

Jeremy Millar

Afterword

Had Sebald continued south along the beach at Dunwich during the dog days of 1992, rather than cutting inland past the monastery and onto the heath, he would have passed the site where, some twenty-four years previously, Jonathan Miller had filmed a scene for his BBC TV adaptation of M.R. James' 1903 story 'Oh, Whistle, and I'll Come to You, My Lad'. In Miller's rather loose relating of this tale, Michael Hordern plays Professor Parker, a curious academic, somewhat reminiscent of a sagging knap-sack incontinently spilling its burden of tics and mumblings. While taking a short winter break in an East Anglian guesthouse, the professor eschews the rather forced companionship of a round on the links, and takes a walk along the beach whereupon he stumbles across a graveyard scarcely clinging to the disintegrating cliff-top. Peering more closely at the precarious stones, he finds a small bone object secreted amongst the earth and grass and, pocketing it, he makes his way back to his lodging, his return shadowed by a mysterious dark figure that follows him along the beach at an agitated distance.

It is not known whether Sebald knew Miller's film, or the story on which it was based, and one can only speculate as to what his feelings would have been towards the Cambridge antiquarian who was its author; perhaps the unsuspecting irruption of anxiety, however caused and however defined, within an environment of placid contentment is something that would have him brought a clouded satisfaction. The literary device so often used by James, of a seemingly inanimate object acting as a means of summoning the past, or its spirits—as the small bone object, a whistle, does so terrifyingly when blown by the professor—of acting as a form of transport to other times or other places, or to other states of mind, now seems itself strangely Sebaldian; numerous are the times—and this happens in Ruskin too—when his collected contemplation of an object, or a scene, gathers together the thoughts, the memories, or the imaginings of other places and times, and of people too, and suddenly they are before us and we know not quite how. Imagine what spectres of history Sebald himself could have brought forth had he found that whistle amongst the Dunwich graves and, with hands now trembling, revealed its Latin inscription —QUIS EST ISTE QUI VENIT—flanked by a pair of swastikas.

Sebald himself might have chosen from a couple of words to describe such curiosity: *neugierde*, or 'greed for the new', is the more recent coinage and, given its obvious emphasis upon novelty, may have been an unlikely choice for one so self-consciously old-fashioned; *fürwitz* is the older, and has connotations of unseemly haste, especially in matters that do not concern one. This latter sense of a curiosity that is, at best, morally ambiguous, is one that can be found throughout the history of Western thought, from the Greeks onwards. The most forceful attack upon such curiosity, however, was made by Augustine who considered it a form of impiety, a distraction from God's glory and the salvation that it holds out for us. Such curiosity was a form of pride, a swelling of desire to know that which has no use, and for no other reason than the sake of knowledge itself. In a passage which foreshadows Sebald's own thoughts on 'the night of time' as he makes his way to Dunwich, Augustine writes of the vainglorious abilities of astronomers who can 'foresee an eclipse of the sun far in the future but even in the present do not see their own eclipse'. James' stories, also, can be similarly admonitory in tone and act: that marked whistle was eventually thrown into the sea where it could bring no further misfortune while another story, concerned also with the tragedy brought on by archaeological finds along the East Anglian coast and written some twenty-two years later, was plainly titled 'A Warning to the Curious'.

The travel books of the medieval period were compendia of wonders, the majority of which were not witnessed by the writer, as claimed, but rather compiled from biblical or other sources (unsurprising considering their development from the Classical genre of paradoxology, in which examples of the abnormal or inexplicable were similarly assembled). Such marvels were considered most common at the world's end, as 'Nature plays with greater freedom secretly at the edges of the world than she does openly and nearer us in the middle of it', an opinion expressed by the fourteenth-century English monk Ranulph Higden, and one shared more widely. An awareness of being on the edge is something that still defines the east of England to this day, as is apparent to anyone who has spent time there, although its isolation is not that imagined some six centuries past. Yet this liminal quality pervades the region, as it pervades Sebald's writing upon it, a sense that thresholds are being moved over—geographic, historic, and artistic, certainly, and perhaps personal most especially—and that these states are as changeable as the shoreline itself. For Sebald himself, it is perhaps curiosity that begins this process, and it continues without rest or satisfaction; indeed, *pace* James, and Augustine well before him, Sebald's curiosity is one of perpetual movement that, like his searching sentences, can seem without end. If there is any sense of conclusion, however, it is neither tragic nor monstrous, although it is certainly remarkable. It is easy to describe *The Rings of Saturn* as a wonderful book; it would be better described as a book of wonder.

Installation photographs at Norwich Castle Museum & Art Gallery and at Sainsbury Centre for the Visual Arts (top middle and bottom right).

Norwich Castle photographs feature cast of the skull of Thomas Browne (Norfolk and Norwich University Hospital NHS Trust) and Pattern Book, late 18th century (Bridewell Museum, Norwich) as referred to in *The Rings of Saturn*.

Norwich Castle photographs
© Brada Barassi

Sainsbury Centre photographs
© Andy Crouch

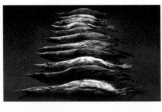 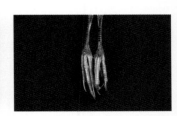

16
Simon Pope: from
The Memorial Walks
2007
Photography © Simon Pope

25
Simon Pope: from
The Memorial Walks
2007
Photography © Simon Pope

26/27
Britain's Bitterns, circa 1997
2007
Photography © Mike Harrington

28
Britain's Bitterns, circa 1997
2007
Photography © Mike Harrington

28
Britain's Bitterns, circa 1997
2007
Photography © Mike Harrington

28
Britain's Bitterns, circa 1997
2007
Photography © Mike Harrington

28
Britain's Bitterns, circa 1997
2007
Photography © Mike Harrington

29
Britain's Bitterns, circa 1997
2007
Photography © Mike Harrington

Britain's Bitterns, circa 1997
(population 11 breeding males)
Written and performed by
Marcus Coates

We were born before the wind,
we taught the reed to sway.
In all the fen I need no friend
I'll have my loves to lay.

As I work the channel edge
I'll feel the sun once more;
wren, water rail and reed bunting
you'll sing the summer raw.

I live to stand and stalk my prey
I am a patient man;
I wait and hunt like this all day
our way in God's good plan.

In all the world you want it new,
you drain our land of plenty;
you'll hear our call no more, for you
the east wind will bear empty.

Where once the wet sky covered soil
so dry and sparse the reeds now stand.
Our fathers' prize here for their toil,
the good few here that are now damned.

You know us like you see the air,
so tell me how long have we now?
So special, Oh, so bloody rare,
we'll do a dance then take a bow.

Come close and I'll point to the sky;
no more to you I'll be the reed.
Once caught and cooked for the pie,
now for the beets I'll sweetly bleed.

As I stab fish and spear the frog, why?
Small sharp mouths must feed.
I'd just as well spear your right eye,
what's left will see your greed.

Some say it all will end with us.
If I knew that I'd end it now.
No flight or fight or sorry fuss,
just one more body for the plough.

Where lies our hope? In you, blue sky!
A sailor's jacket, perhaps?
The sun might smile, but while we die
you'll breed that debt no doubt.

I'll ne'er leave this my shrinking land,
mine is the deepest cry;
breed and feed from my rich hand,
Oh come to me my loves and die.

Note
The Bittern is a large secretive bird,
related to the heron. Its striped
brown plumage creates an effective
camouflage making it a very difficult
bird to see in its dense reedbed habitat.

Bitterns adopt a 'skypointing'
camouflaged position with their neck
and body fully stretched vertically,
the bill pointing upwards and eyes
swivelled forwards, blending in with the
reed stems. While in this position birds
have been known to sway, micking the
movement of the reeds in the wind.

Male bitterns are polygamous, covering
a number of females across a large
territory.

Bitterns walk slowly and deliberately,
and may stand motionless for some
time stalking fish and amphibians.

The bittern's dependence on reedbeds
and its very small population make it
a Red List species—one of the most
threatened in the UK. In 1997, there
were only 11 male bitterns calling in the
UK, Norfolk being a stronghold.

Loss and impoverishment of the reed
habitat through drainage for agricultural
uses has contributed to the sustained
decline of the species in the UK.

The males make a booming sound in
spring which is the lowest-pitched and
the most far-carrying song produced
by any European bird—up to 5km in
the right weather.

Its traditional name of 'Butterbump'
refers to the fat deposits on the birds
rump which has historically made it a
source of food for humans.

Weather folklore: If there's enough blue
sky to make a sailor's jacket the day
will be fine.

40/41
Michael Hamburger
location photograph
2007
Photography © Tacita Dean

42
Michael Hamburger
installation photograph
2007
Photography © Brada Barassi

43
Michael Hamburger
installation photograph
2007
Photography © Brada Barassi

Michael Hamburger, 2007
16mm colour anamorphic film, optical sound, 28 minutes

With Michael Hamburger and Anne Beresford

Director of Photography
Jamie Cairney

Camera Operator
Tom Wright

Sound Recordist
Annie Needham

Clapper Loaders
Rob Hart and Amy Newstead

Sound Editors
James Harrison; Steve Felton

Digital Sound Post Production
The Sound Design Company,
with thanks to Steve Felton

Telecine
Arion

Neg Cut
Reelskill

Optical Sound Transfer
Martin Sawyer Sound Services

Printed by
Soho Images, with thanks to
Len Thornton

Originated on
Kodak Motion Picture Film

With special thanks to Jane Hamlyn
and Anne Beresford.

With thanks to John Adderley,
Jeremy Millar, Steven Bode, Nina Ernst
and Kenneth Graham.

Filmed on location in Middleton, Suffolk

Courtesy of
Frith Street Gallery, London
and Marian Goodman Gallery,
New York/Paris

43
Michael Hamburger
installation photograph
2007
Photography © Brada Barassi

44
Michael Hamburger
installation photograph
2007
Photography © Brada Barassi

44
Michael Hamburger
installation photograph
2007
Photography © Brada Barassi

44
Michael Hamburger
installation photograph
2007
Photography © Brada Barassi

45
Michael Hamburger
location photograph
2007
Photography © Tacita Dean

46/47
Michael Hamburger
location photograph
2007
Photography © Tacita Dean

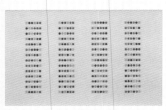

48/49

fall (for Michael Hamburger)
2007
Photography © Maris

50/51

Circle poem (letting go)
Circle poem (what changes change)
2007

52/53

Circle poem (with our back)
Circle poem (after Debussy)
2007

54

Bell Method (Plain Bob Minor), detail
2007
Photography © Bevis Bowden

55

Bell Method (Plain Bob Minor),
installation photograph
2007
Photography © Andy Crouch 2007

57

The Ruins 1, Walberswick
2007

Note
Dunwich was a prosperous seaport,
and third largest town in East Anglia;
on the night of 14th January 1328, a
storm threw a shingle bank across the
harbour mouth, ruining the shipping
and fishing industries. Instead,
prosperity passed up the coast, to the
village at the mouth of the new inlet.
This was Walberswick.

Walberswick Parish Church already
existed at the time of the 1328 storm.
Indeed, a church existed here at the
time of Domesday, 1085. We know
a lot about it, because, incredibly, the
15th Century parish minutes survived.
We know that it was a thatched
church, but that it probably had a tower
because there were bells.

(from www.suffolkchurches.co.uk)

All Saints Church: last of Dunwich's
ancient churches to be lost to the sea.
All Saints was abandoned in the 1750s.
It reached the cliff's edge in 1904 with
the tower falling in 1922.

St Bartholomew's: one of two
'Domesday' churches, thought to have
been lost in the storm of 1328.

St John the Baptist: Dunwich's leading
church throughout the Middle Ages.
In 1510 a pier was erected in an
attempt to act as a breakwater from
the sea and in 1542 further funds were
raised in a bid to save the building
but to no avail and the building was
largely demolished before it went over
the cliffs.

St Martin's: Built before 1175, it was
lost to the sea between 1335 and
1408.

St Michael's: The other 'Domesday'
church, it was lost to the sea in the
storm of 1328.

Other Dunwich churches lost to the
sea include: St Leonard's, thought
to have been abandoned soon after
the Black Death, probably lost to the
sea soon afterwards; St Nicholas:
lost to the sea soon after the Black
Death; St Peter's, east gable fell in
1688 and the rest of the building
followed in 1697; Preceptory of the
Knights Templar, demolished following
the dissolution of the Hospitallers in
1562, the foundations washed away
during the reign of Charles I; St Francis
Chapel, lost in the 16th century; St
Anthony's Chapel, lost around 1330;
St Katherine's Chapel, lost in the
16th century; The Benedictine Cell,
attached to Ely Cathedral and lost
during the storm of 1328; Blackfriars
Dominican priory, the last building
recorded as having fallen to the sea
in 1717; Greyfriars Franciscan priory,
abandoned due to the advancing
sea in 1328, rebuilt further inland, the
ruins survive to this day, although the
encroaching cliffs are now but a few
hundred feet away.

Guy Moreton

With additional thanks to the Henry Moore Foundation and Southampton Solent University.

58/59
The River Yare 1
2007

60/61
The River Yare 2
2007

62/63
Dingle Marsh, Dunwich
2007

64/65
Dunston Pillar
detail
2007

69

S.W. Fitt: Eccles By Sea
c. 1890
© Norfolk County Council Library
and Information Service

Note

In the early seventeenth century, the Norfolk village of Eccles by the Sea was inundated with the loss of seventy houses and three-hundred lives. In the years that followed, the church, which had survived the storm, was overthrown by the remaining inhabitants unable afford its upkeep. The steeple alone was left free-standing, and by the early nineteenth century it stood, just, on the landward side of the dunes. As the sea continued its advance, the dunes were pushed ever back onto the old tower, by the 1850s burying all but its highest window beneath the sand. By the 1880s the steeple was down on the beach, a landmark to passing ships until its collapse in a storm of 23 January 1895. Ernest R. Suffling, a local writer, captured its final hours:

On January 22nd, 1895, a windy but bright day, I strolled on the beach after lunch, and requiring a light for my pipe entered the old tower and obtained one. Then, standing with my back against the leeside, I watched the shadow of the steeple glide almost imperceptibly over the ribbed sand. For 290 years the old tower had served as a beacon, but I little dreamed that I was the last person who should stand in its shade. Yet so it was, for the 23rd broke stormily, and the sea, even at low tide, prevented any one from entering the doorway. As the tide rose the tower received the full force of both sea and gale. I watched the great waves breaking in thunder and bombarding the tower with timber, piles, and planks from the demolished breakwaters, and lingered until I could no longer see. Between 6 and 7 o'clock p.m. the tower fell, but no one actually saw its fall, nor even heard it, so great was the fury of the storm. On the 24th many persons came to see the fallen patriarch, and each, with myself, agreed that it seemed like standing beside a dead friend, when we gazed upon this well-known link with the past lying prostrate before us.

The Land of the Broads, 1895

Alexander & Susan Maris

Silentium, 2007
*High-definition video,
26 minutes*

Artist/Directors
Alexander & Susan Maris

Cinematographer
Bevis Bowden

First Camera Assistant
Brada Barassi

Sound Engineer
Ross Adams

Post Production
Pepper Post

With special thanks to
Steven Bode, Jeremy Millar and
everyone at Film and Video Umbrella,
Donny and Marian Brown, Don Brown,
Ruth Hawkins and David Nicholson,
Sarah Lucas, Alan Wright and the
crew of the *Shelley*.

70/71
Silentium
film still
2007

72/73
Silentium
film still
2007

74
Silentium
film still
2007

74
Silentium
film still
2007

74/75
Silentium
film still
2007

76/77
Silentium
film still
2007

Simon Pope

84/85
from The Memorial Walks
2007
Photography © Brada Barassi

87
The Memorial Walks
(after James Stark/
Marlborough Forest)
2007
Photography © Mike Harrington

87
The Memorial Walks
(after John Crome/Grove Scene)
2007
Photography © Mike Harrington

87
The Memorial Walks
(after John Berney Ladbrooke/
The Great Oak)
2007
Photography © Mike Harrington

87
The Memorial Walks
(after John Sell Cotman/
The Silent Stream, Normandy)
2007
Photography © Mike Harrington

87
The Memorial Walks
(after Frederick Mackenzie/Monks
Lane, Lincoln)
2007
Photography © Bevis Bowden

87
The Memorial Walks
(after Henry Bright/Grove Scene)
2007
Photography © Mike Harrington

88
from The Memorial Walks
2007
Photography © Simon Pope

89
from The Memorial Walks
2007
Photography © Simon Pope

Walkers

Rex Hancy
Drayton to the River Wensum Valley

George Szirtes
Upton to Upton Marshes

Marjorie Allthorpe-Guyton
Acle to Acle Bridge via
Hermitage Marshes

Amanda Hopkinson
South Walsham Broad

Tom McCarthy
Acle to Acle Bridge

Hari Kunzru
Cantley to Reedham

Sean French & Nicci Gerrard
Haddiscoe towards Reedham Ferry

Brian Dillon
Postwick Marshes

Ken Worpole
Rockland Marsh

Trezza Azzopardi
Upton Staithe

Geoff Dyer
Potterhanworth Wood to Fox's Drain

Sally O'Reilly
Neville Wood to Nocton Fen

Stuart Jeffries
Potterhanworth Booths to
Langham Drain

90

The Memorial Walks
(after Samuel David Colkett/
Landscape with cows in a pool
by a clump of trees)
2007
Photography © Mike Harrington

91

The Memorial Walks
(after Henry Bright/Grove Scene)
2007
Photography © Mike Harrington

Tacita Dean

W.G. Sebald
92
Map found by Joseph Dean
in Goch, 1944.
Photo: J. Littkemann

93
Found photographs of Goch, 1944.

93
Goch, 2003.
Photos: Dr. Georg Kersting

94
Photographs of the bombing of
Goch, taken from the Steenbeck
of the film, *Krieg am Niederrhein*
by Heinz Bosch and Wilhelm Haas,
1981.
Courtesy Imperial War Museum
and Kreis Kleve

95
Tacita Dean in the bus stop,
Naselesele, Fiji.
Photo: Mathew Hale

96
Katy English in the drawing room
of Glendun Lodge.
Photo: Philip English

96
Exterior of Glendun Lodge.
Photo: Philip English

97
Postcard from Murlough Bay,
Co. Antrim.
© Ulster Card Company Ltd

98
Roger Casement in the dock
at Bow Street Court, May 1916.
Drawing by F. Matania.
© Getty Images, Hulton Archive

99
Rufus Isaacs, 1st Marquess of
Reading. Photograph by Walton
Adams, 1910.
© Rosalind Adams, with thanks to
the National Portrait Gallery, London

99
Reverse side of the Hulton archive
Roger Casement photograph.
© Getty Images, Hulton Archive

100
*Rufus Isaacs, 1st Marquess of
Reading*, painting by William
Orpen, 1919.
Courtesy National Portrait Gallery,
London

102
Picture of Godfrey Isaacs from
Mayfair Magazine, October 9th,
1915.
© Marconi Corporation plc

102
Godfrey Isaacs and Mrs Isaacs in
Chelmsford, 15th June 1920.
© Marconi Corporation plc

103
Guglielmo Marconi with Godfrey
Isaacs attending the court enquiry
into the disaster of the sinking of
the *Titanic*, 1912.
© Marconi Corporation plc

104/105
National Cabinet Group, August
31st, 1931. Photographs by
James Jarché.
© Science & Society Picture Library

106
Intérieur du Café Carrel, Arles by
Vincent Van Gogh, Arles, August
1888. Oil on canvas.
Courtesy of James Roundell, London

109
The Presentation of the Heine
Prize to W.G. Sebald in the Senate
Room of County Hall in the City of
Düsseldorf by the Mayor Joachim
Erwin on December 13th, 2000.
Photo: Wilfried Meyer

With thanks to:
Joseph Dean, Winton Dean and
Stephen Dean, Guido de Werd,
Rita Kersting, Dr. Radegund &
Dr. Georg Kersting, Katy English,
Monique Hageman from the Van
Gogh Museum, Louise Jamison of
the Marconi Archive.

'W.G. Sebald' was first published
as part of *Seven Books* to
accompany Dean's exhibition at
Musée d'Art Moderne de la Ville
de Paris, May 7–June 22, 2003.
Published by Steidl, Germany.

Notes on Contributors

Steven Bode is Director of Film and Video Umbrella. During his fifteen years in that role, he has curated numerous artists' film and video projects, as well as other exhibitions, such as 'Airport' (with Jeremy Millar), 'The Other Side of Zero' (for Video Positive, Liverpool) and 'New Video from Great Britain' (for MoMA, New York).

———

Marcus Coates' practice questions how we perceive humanness through non-human realities. Coates studied at the Royal Academy of Arts, 1990–93. Recent solo exhibitions include 'Marcus Coates', Whitechapel Gallery, London 2007 and 'Dawn Chorus', Baltic Centre for Contemporary Art, Gateshead 2007. Coates has recently staged performances at Hayward Gallery, London 2007, Arnolfini, Bristol 2007, Tokyo and Stavanger, Norway 2006.

———

Brian Dillon is the author of a memoir, *In the Dark Room* (Penguin, 2005). He is UK editor of *Cabinet* magazine, and his writing has appeared in *Frieze*, *Art Review*, the *London Review of Books*, the *Times Literary Supplement*, *Sight & Sound* and *The Wire*. He lives in Canterbury.

———

Tacita Dean works in a variety of media: film, sound, drawings and objects. She is best known for her compelling 16mm films, in which the specific qualities associated with film-making are of central importance. Dean won the Hugo Boss award in 2006 and recently had a solo exhibition at Dublin's Hugh Lane Gallery. The largest exhibition of her work was staged at Schaulager, Basel in 2006. Other notable exhibitions include Museum of Art, Design and Architecture Oslo, Tate Britain and Musee d'art moderne de la ville de Paris.

———

Alec Finlay is an artist, poet and publisher. He is currently working on 'w/m', a residency at the National Centre for Renewable Energy (Blyth) and 'Specimen Colony', a public artwork and book for Bluecoat Gallery (Liverpool). Recent publications include *Ludwig Wittgenstein: There Where You Are Not* (Black Dog), *Mesostic Laboratorium* (platform projects), *Thought-Cloud Jotter* (Science Learning Centre) and *a slower shower* (island). He lives and works in Byker, Newcastle-upon-Tyne.

———

Matthew Hollis was born in Norwich in 1971. *Ground Water* (Bloodaxe 2004), his first full-length collection, was shortlisted for the Whitbread Prize for Poetry, the Guardian First Book Award and the Forward Prize for Best First Collection. He is co-editor of *101 Poems Against War* (Faber, 2003) and *Strong Words: Modern Poets on Modern Poetry* (Bloodaxe, 2000), and works as an editor at Faber and Faber.

———

Robert Macfarlane was born in Oxford in 1976. His *Mountains of the Mind* (Granta: 2003) won the Guardian First Book Award and a Somerset Maugham Award. *The Wild Places*, a journey in search of wildness in Britain and Ireland, is published by Granta in autumn 2007. He is presently writing an unconventional biography of W.G. Sebald. He is a Fellow of Emmanuel College, Cambridge.

———

Alexander & Susan Maris describe themselves as 'Post-Urban' artists, and have been collaborating as such since 1990. They are currently working on a digitally archived reforestation project for Rannoch Moor, which anticipates the eventual reintroduction of the European Wolf, Lynx and Black Bear into the Highlands of Scotland.

———

Jeremy Millar is an artist and currently AHRC Research Fellow in the Creative and Performing Arts at the University of Oxford. A contributor to *Searching for Sebald* (ICI, 2007), he is author, with Tacita Dean, of *Place* (Thames and Hudson, 2005), and of *The Way Things Go* (Afterall Books, 2007).

———

Guy Moreton is an artist and photographer. His work has been published and exhibited internationally, notably at Whitechapel Gallery, London, Kettle's Yard, Cambridge, EAST International, Norwich, and John Hansard Gallery, University of Southampton. He is co-author with Alec Finlay and Michael Nedo of *Ludwig Wittgenstein: There Where You Are Not* published by Black Dog London. He is a senior lecturer in the School of Visual Arts, Southampton Solent University.

———

Simon Pope was born in Exeter in 1966. In 2002 he was awarded a NESTA Fellowship to investigate walking as a contemporary art practice, and represented Wales at their inaugural exhibition at the Venice Biennale of Fine Art 2003. He curated the touring exhibition, 'Art for Networks', (2001–3), and is the author of *London Walking* (Ellipsis, 2000). Previous work includes the collaborative software project, 'IOD 4: The Web Stalker' (2000).

———

George Szirtes was born in Budapest in 1948. Trained as an artist, he has written some dozen books of poetry that have won the Faber Prize, the Cholmondeley Award and been short-listed for The Whitbread Prize. His most recent book *Reel* (Bloodaxe, 2004) was a PBS Choice and was awarded the T.S. Eliot Prize in 2005.

He met Max Sebald shortly after moving to East Anglia, dedicating his long poem, 'Backwaters: Norfolk Fields' (in *An English Apocalypse*, Bloodaxe 2001) to Sebald while he was alive. After Sebald's death he published another long poem, 'Meeting Austerlitz' (in *Reel*, 2004) as a commemoration.

———

Waterlog

Waterlog: Journeys Around An Exhibition
Edited by Steven Bode,
Jeremy Millar and Nina Ernst
Designed by SampsonMay

In Memoriam
Michael Hamburger 1924–2007
Elsbeth Bode 1913–2007
Ruth Millar 1924–2007

With thanks to Arts Council England,
the Henry Moore Foundation,
Norwich Castle Museum & Art Gallery,
Sainsbury Centre for Visual Arts and
The Collection, Lincoln.

Film and Video Umbrella
8 Vine Yard
London SE1 1QL
Tel: 020 7407 7755
info@fvu.co.uk

www.waterlog.fvu.co.uk